T0380978

To order additional copies of this book, contact:
Xlibris
1-888-795-4274
www.Xlibris.com
Orders@Xlibris.com

FOXY
DO RIGHT
Don't Talk to Strangers

Foxy waved goodbye as she left for school. Mother Fox warned, "Don't talk to strangers Foxy."

"I know, I know. Later mom, later dad." Mother Fox watches as Foxy heads down the hill to school.

On the way to school, Foxy kicks the rocks and swings her backpack. "It will be a great day at school today." Foxy whistles along and notices a Big Fox walking in her direction. This fox was an older, nice-looking fox holding a paper bag.

The Big Fox stopped and said, "Hey little Foxy, want some candy?" Foxy, startled by the Big Fox, kept walking. "Don't talk to strangers," she thought to herself.

The Big Fox repeated, "Hey little Foxy! Would you like some candy?" Foxy liked candy, especially the kind you can wear as jewelry. Those were her favorite. Foxy didn't know what to do. She loved candy oh so very much.

Foxy stopped. What should Foxy do? Foxy yelled out, "Don't talk to strangers!" and sprinted off as fast as she could.

With the Big Fox no longer near, Foxy slowed down to catch her breath.

She saw an Old Lady Fox calling for her pet. "Sampson, ole Sampson where are you? Hello little Foxy can you help me find my little Sampson?" The Old Lady Fox looked harmless and Foxy didn't want her to lose her pet. What should Foxy do?

Foxy sprinted off running and yelling, "Don't talk to strangers!"

Foxy could see her school in sight. She ran faster and darted in the building just in time for the bell to ring.

"Good morning class," sang Mrs. Foxtail. The class sang back, "Good morning Mrs. Foxtail." "I'm glad you all are here today. Pull out your books and write." Foxy thought about all the things she could write about before she knew it the bell rung for recess.

"Alright class, it is time for recess. Let's go," Mrs. Foxtail reminded.

All the little foxes ran out to the playground and climbed, jumped and raced. Foxy swung. She heard a faint whistling sound.

Foxy looked around and by the fence stood a Sly Fox dressed in a black suit with a hat and a gold watch dangling from his pocket.

As he tossed a coin in the air he called, "Hey little Foxy, come to the fence and talk. I got a secret to tell you." Foxy liked secrets but Foxy also knew this fox was up to no good. What should Foxy do?

Foxy jumped off the swing in midair yelling, "Don't talk to strangers!"

Foxy ran to her Teacher Mrs. Foxtail and pointed. "Mrs. Foxtail! There's a stranger!" Mrs. Foxtail looked to where Foxy was pointing but no fox was in sight. Mrs. Foxtail gathered all the little foxes, and they headed back inside.

The school bell rang to end their day and the little foxes grabbed their backpacks to head out. Mrs. Foxtail called Foxy over to her desk. "Thank you Foxy for being so alert when you saw a stranger. It is always best to get in a safe place, tell an adult and don't talk to strangers. Just for that, you are getting two gold stars and you will be our safety officer." Foxy was thrilled.

Foxy headed home with no other fox in sight. As she got home, she could smell her mom baking her favorite treat: fudge brownies. Mom only made these on special occasions or when Foxy did something good. "I wonder what's the special occasion?" Foxy thought.

Foxy ran into the house filled with excitement. "Hey, Foxy you must have had a great day. What's all the excitement about?" Mother Fox asked with a smile. Foxy replied, "I did a great job at school and now I am a safety officer!" "Oh, my!" Mother Fox replied gleefully. "What did you do to earn safety officer?" "Well, momma, I saw a fox that tried to get me to talk to him during recess, but I ran and yelled "Don't talk to strangers!" just like you told me. I told Mrs. Foxtail about him but then he disappeared."

"That is a great and smart thing to do Foxy. Be careful. Go clean yourself up and tell Father Fox it is time for dinner." "Ok, mom," Foxy replied. Foxy scurried off to put away her things.

"Father Fox," she called out, "it is time to eat."

As Foxy entered the room, Father Fox was in the closet putting things away in a chest.

He hurriedly closed the chest as Foxy approached. "Well, hello my dear sweet foxy. How was school today?"

Foxy told Father Fox about her day as they headed to the kitchen.

Foxy noticed a dangling gold watch from Father Fox's side pocket. She pointed and asked, "Where did you get that from? It looks familiar." Father Fox replied, "It was a gift from my father, your Grandpa Fox."

Foxy stopped and said, "No Father Fox, it looks just like the gold watch that the Sly Fox was wearing."

As they sat for supper Father Fox explained. "You are correct Foxy; I am glad you noticed." Foxy looked confused.

"Today when you headed off to school, I was the fox with the candy, and I was the sly fox at the fence. I wanted to make sure you would not talk to strangers as your mother and I have taught you." Foxy looked shocked as she tried to understand what Father fox had just told her.

"So, you're telling me that the strangers, were you?" "That's right Foxy," said Father Fox. Foxy interrupted, "But wait you mean to tell me you were the Old Lady Fox also?" Mother Fox giggled, "Oh no Foxy that was me in her little old lady voice." Father Fox interrupted, "Although this time it was us, it may not be again.

That's why it's so important to be safe and..."
Foxy yelled "Don't talk to strangers! Now, who's
up for some dessert?" Foxy smiles gleefully as
she nibbles on her treat.

The end.

Printed in the United States
By Bookmasters